Hearing

A Troll Question Book™

By Kathie Billingslea Smith & Victoria Crenson
Illustrated by Robert S. Storms
Medical Consultant: Ira T. Fine, M.D.

Library of Congress Cataloging in Publication Data

Smith, Kathie Billingslea.
  Hearing.

  (A Troll question book)
    Summary: Questions and answers provide basic
information about hearing and the ear, covering such
topics as "Can I hear things when I'm asleep?" and "How
do I take care of my ears?"
    1. Hearing—Juvenile literature. [1. Hearing.
2. Ear. 3. Questions and answers] I. Crenson, Victoria.
II. Storms, Robert S., ill. III. Title.
QP462.2.S65   1988   612'.85   87-5854
ISBN 0-8167-1006-6 (lib. bdg.)
ISBN 0-8167-1007-4 (pbk.)

Troll Associates
Mahwah, N.J.

What is sound?

Stretch a rubber band between your fingers. Snap it with your other hand. Can you see the rubber band moving back and forth very quickly? It is vibrating. Sounds are vibrations that move through the air.

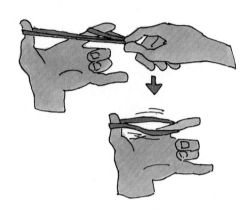

When you clap your hands or stamp your feet, vibrations, or sound waves, travel out in bigger and bigger circles like ripples in a puddle when a stone is thrown in it.

Sound waves vibrate at different speeds. The faster a wave vibrates, the higher the sound heard. The sound wave for a car horn might look like this:〰〰. But the low purr of the car engine might look like this: 〜〜〜.

In your throat are vocal chords that vibrate and make sounds when you talk or sing. Sing in a high voice and the vocal chords vibrate very quickly. Sing a low note and they vibrate more slowly.

What are the parts

There are three main parts to your ear — the outer ear, the middle ear, and the inner ear.

The outer ear, or *pinna*, is the part that is visible. It is made of skin and soft bone and can be bent easily. The pinna acts like a funnel. It directs sounds into the ear canal. This passageway leads to the *eardrum*. This is a sheet of skin or *membrane* that is stretched across the entrance

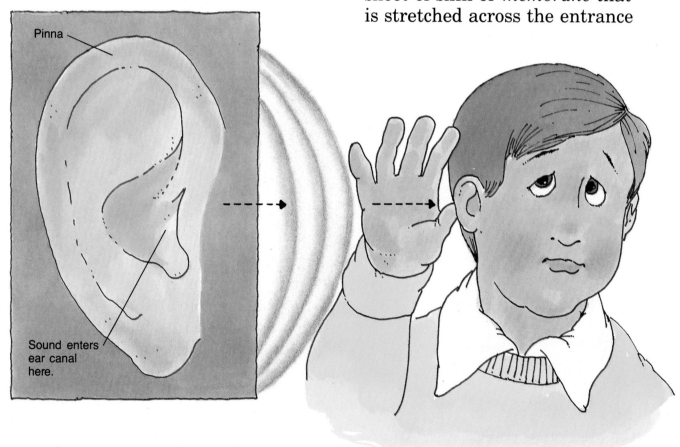

Pinna

Sound enters ear canal here.

# of my ear?

to the middle ear.

The middle ear has three tiny bones — the *hammer*, the *anvil*, and the *stirrup* — that form a bridge between the eardrum and the inner ear.

Inside the inner ear is a coiled tube called the *cochlea*. It looks like a snail's shell and is filled with fluid and nerve endings. The inner ear also has three looped tubes called the *semicircular canals*. These help control balance.

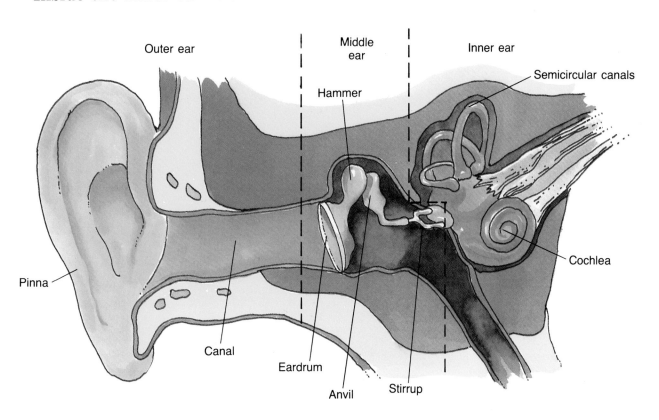

When a sound is made, the outer ear, or pinna, helps direct the sound waves into the ear canal. Energy from the sound makes the eardrum vibrate just like a bass drum. These vibrations become stronger as they pass through the three bones of the middle ear to the cochlea in the inner ear. Special nerves in the cochlea carry the sound signals to a certain part of the brain.

The brain compares the

1. Sound wave goes to ear canal.

2. Eardrum vibrates.

hear?

sounds with other memories stored there. It helps you understand what you have heard. For example, when your brain receives a signal for a ringing sound, it compares the sound with other ringing tones you have heard before. Then the brain lets you know whether you are hearing the telephone or the doorbell or a school bell or an ice-cream bell! This all happens very quickly.

RING!

RING!

5. Sound wave tells brain what kind of sound.

4. Sound wave carries signal to cochlea.

3. Sound wave passes signal to anvil. (and hammer and stirrup)

AN ICE-CREAM BELL

ICE CREAM

6. Brain lets you know what sound you heard.

Can I hear things

Different sounds are always being made around you — even at night when everything seems quiet and you are sound asleep. Clocks *tick-tock, tick-tock* all night long. Birds chirp outside the window. Cars drive by your house. Perhaps your father snores. *ZZZZzzzzz!*

Z-Z-Z-Z-z-z-z

TICK TOCK!

TICK TOCK!

Z-Z-Z-Z-Z-Z-Z-Z-Z-Z-Z

when I'm asleep?

All of these sounds travel through your ears and send messages to your brain. But you do not hear all of the sounds. A special part of the brain screens the incoming messages. It only sends on those that seem important or unusual. Most night sounds are normal ones that are heard often. Your brain blocks them out and does not have you wake up to hear them.

But unusual or important sounds — such as a telephone or a fire alarm — are sent right to the thinking part of the brain so that you can hear them and wake up.

Why do my ears "pop"

Ears feel most comfortable when the air outside the eardrum is the same pressure as the air inside the eardrum. But when your body goes up or down quickly, the air pressure outside the eardrum changes. This can happen in an elevator, on an airplane, or driving in the mountains. For a short time, the change in elevation may make your ears hurt a little and keep you from hearing normally.

This problem can be fixed simply by yawning or swallowing! How? When you yawn or swallow, the *eustachian tube* — the tube that connects the throat with the middle ear — opens up and lets air in or out of the ear. This makes a "popping" sound in your head. Then the air pressure is the same on both sides of the

ELEVATION 14000 FEET

in an airplane?

eardrum, and you feel better.

Flight attendants on airplanes suggest that passengers chew gum during takeoffs and landings. This helps the passenger swallow more often, thereby opening the eustachian tube and keeping the ears from hurting.

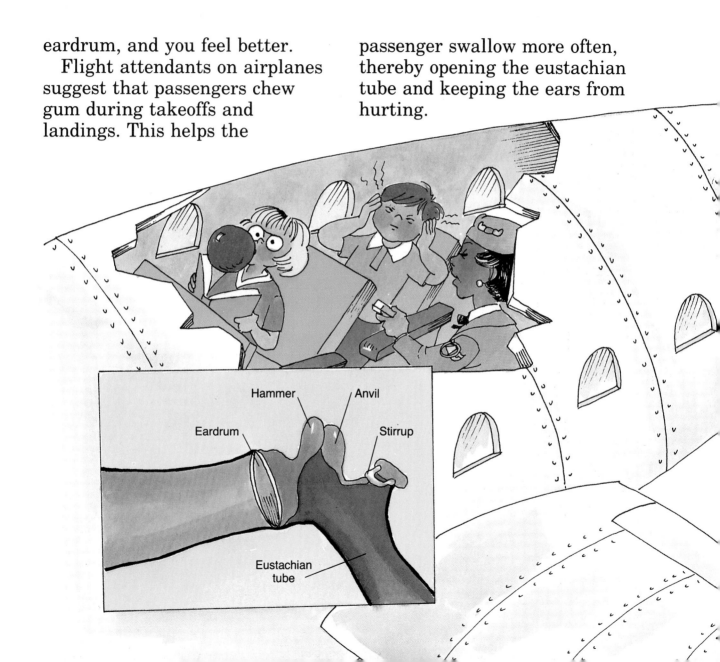

Eardrum

Hammer

Anvil

Stirrup

Eustachian tube

Can everyone hear?

No, there are people who cannot hear. They cannot talk on the telephone, hear a baby laugh, or listen to music. Everything is quiet to them. They are deaf.

There are also people who suffer from a hearing loss. For these people, listening to the world is like listening to a radio with the volume turned down. Everything sounds far away to them. But they may be helped by wearing hearing aids.

Hearing aids are like tiny microphones that fit inside or

Hearing aid

behind the ears. The hearing aids pick up sounds to make them louder. Then they play the sounds into the ears so that the hard of hearing can hear better.

Another kind of hearing loss makes the world sound as if you turned a radio station dial a little bit off the station. The sound is fuzzy: you can hear voices, but you can't always make out what they are saying. Hearing aids are not much help for these people.

How do deaf people

Most deaf people learn to talk with their hands, using *sign language*. That means they make pictures or signs with their hands to show different words or ideas. Deaf people can also talk by spelling words with their fingers. They arrange their fingers in special ways that

represent letters of the alphabet and spell out what they want to say.

Many deaf people can read lips as well. They carefully look at your lips when you are talking and try to understand what you are saying.

If you knock on the door or

communicate?

ring the doorbell of a deaf person's home, a Hearing Ear dog can alert its owner that someone is at the door. Hearing Ear dogs are specially trained dogs that can tell deaf people about sounds they cannot hear, like the morning alarm clock ringing. Hearing Ear dogs act as ears for their deaf owners.

Most mammals, fish, and insects can hear very well. In fact, some of them can hear better than people can!

Dogs can hear very high notes that people can't. If you were to blow a silent dog whistle, very high-pitched notes would be sounded. You would not hear a thing, but all of the neighborhood dogs would!

When you hear mice squeak, you take notice, but they also communicate with each other in

high-pitched squeaks that the human ear can't hear. Cats, on the other hand, can hear these squeaks and listen for them when they are hunting mice!

animals hear?

Fish have inner ears hidden under their scales. Scientists think that fish understand each other by making different sounds. Skin divers and sailors on submarines claim that fish, whales, and dolphins become quite noisy at night. They make many different sounds to communicate with each other.

Some animals cannot hear at all! Snakes are deaf. They must use other senses to help them survive.

How do instruments

Beat a drum with your hand. You can hear and feel the head of the drum vibrating. Guitars and violins have strings that vibrate when they are plucked or a bow is drawn across them. Blow into a flute, trumpet, or trombone, and the air inside vibrates and out comes a sound. Every musical instrument makes something vibrate.

Without movement there is no sound. And music is a kind of sound.

To make a higher note the string or air must vibrate faster. When a guitarist presses down a string at the neck of the guitar, the string is shortened. Now it vibrates faster, and a higher note is heard. A trombone player can make higher notes by

make music?

sliding the parts of the instrument together. This shortens the trombone so the air has less room and vibrates faster.

Inside a piano there are strings for every key on the keyboard. The keys at the top of the keyboard that play high notes have short strings. The ones at the bottom of the keyboard that sound like thunder have longer strings. When you push down keys, little hammers inside the piano strike the strings and make them vibrate. Out comes beautiful music!

Low notes

High notes

What happens when

Most ear infections take place in the middle ear. They are caused by germs. Often when you have a cold, germs travel from your throat through the eustachian tube to your middle ear. Fluid gathers in the middle ear, and the ear becomes swollen. Then the middle ear bones have trouble moving so that you cannot hear very well. Doctors call this condition *otitis media*, which means "inflammation of the middle ear."

If you have an ear infection,

get an ear infection?

see the doctor. The doctor will use a tool called an *otoscope* to check inside your ears. The otoscope has a light on it to help the doctor look into the eardrum.

The doctor may give you special medicines to clear up an ear infection. The medicines will shrink the ear membranes and dry up the extra fluid. Then you will feel much better!

How do I take care

The first rule of taking care of your ears is never put anything into them! Your eardrums are fragile and could be easily broken.

Go to a doctor if your ears start to hurt. It is important to have your ears checked regularly and the wax removed.

Try to stay away from very loud noises. If a noise is too loud, hold your hands over your ears. Being around too much noise for a long time can damage your ears, causing a hearing loss.

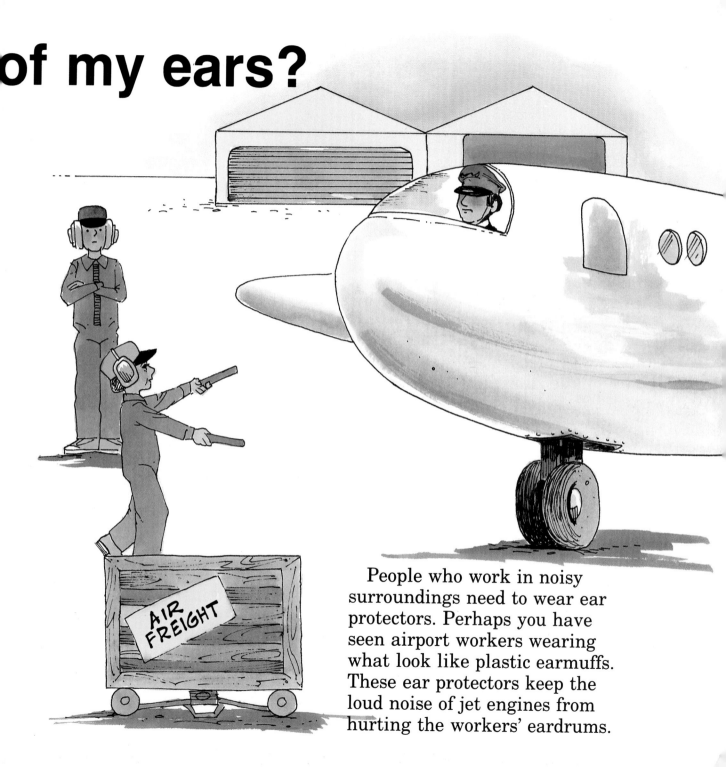

of my ears?

People who work in noisy surroundings need to wear ear protectors. Perhaps you have seen airport workers wearing what look like plastic earmuffs. These ear protectors keep the loud noise of jet engines from hurting the workers' eardrums.

What are the most important sounds I hear?

The most important sounds you hear are words being spoken. Words are not just noises like the sound of a car motor running or the bang of a balloon as it pops. Words have meanings that can be understood by many people. Words represent feelings and thoughts and ideas.

With words, people can communicate, share, teach, explain, learn, and understand.

Words can be spoken . . . or whispered . . . or shouted . . . or sung.

All around you, words are being said. Listen. Listen carefully.